THE STRAWBERRY THIEF

BY ALISON HAWES

ILLUSTRATED BY ANTHONY WILLIAMS

Titles in the Travellers series

Level 3
Goal!	Jane A C West
Too Hot	Roger Hurn/Alison Hawes

Level 4
A Big Catch	Alison Hawes
Deyda's Drum	Roger Hurn
The Strawberry Thief	Alison Hawes
Billy's Boy	Melanie Joyce

Level 5
Cage Boy	Jillian Powell
Master Blasters	Melanie Joyce
Game Player King	Stan Cullimore
In the Zone	Tony Norman

Level 6
Dodgems	Jane A C West
Tansy Smith	Helen Orme

Level 7
Pirate Attack	Jonny Zucker
Hitting the Basket	Jonny Zucker

Badger Publishing Limited
Oldmedow Road, Hardwick Industrial Estate
King's Lynn PE30 4JJ
Telephone: 01438 791037

www.badgerlearning.co.uk

2 4 6 8 10 9 7 5

The Strawberry Thief ISBN 978 1 84691 846 9

First edition © 2010
This second edition © 2014

Text © Alison Hawes 2010
Complete work © Badger Publishing Limited 2010

All rights reserved. No part of this publication may be reproduced, stored in any form or by any means mechanical, electronic, recording or otherwise without the prior permission of the publisher.

The right of Alison Hawes to be identified as author of this Work has been asserted by her in accordance with the Copyright, Designs and Patents Act 1988.

Publisher: David Jamieson
Editor: Danny Pearson
Design: Fiona Grant
Illustration: Anthony Williams

The Strawberry Thief

Contents

Chapter 1
The Farmer   5

Chapter 2
A Light   8

Chapter 3
Thief   12

Questions   16

Badger
LEARNING

Vocabulary:

Strawberry   Portuguese

Cross   Stealing

Thief   Loud

Main characters:

Teresa

Dani

Dad
(Portuguese
migrant worker)

farmer
(owner of
strawberry farm)

Chapter 1
The Farmer

Dad and Mum worked at the strawberry farm.

Sometimes, Dani and Teresa helped them.

One day, the farmer said,
"Someone is stealing my strawberries."

"It's Teresa!" laughed Dani.

"She's eating them all!"

CHAPTER 2
A LIGHT

Teresa was cross with Dani.

The farmer looked cross, too.

One night, it rained.

The noise woke Teresa up.

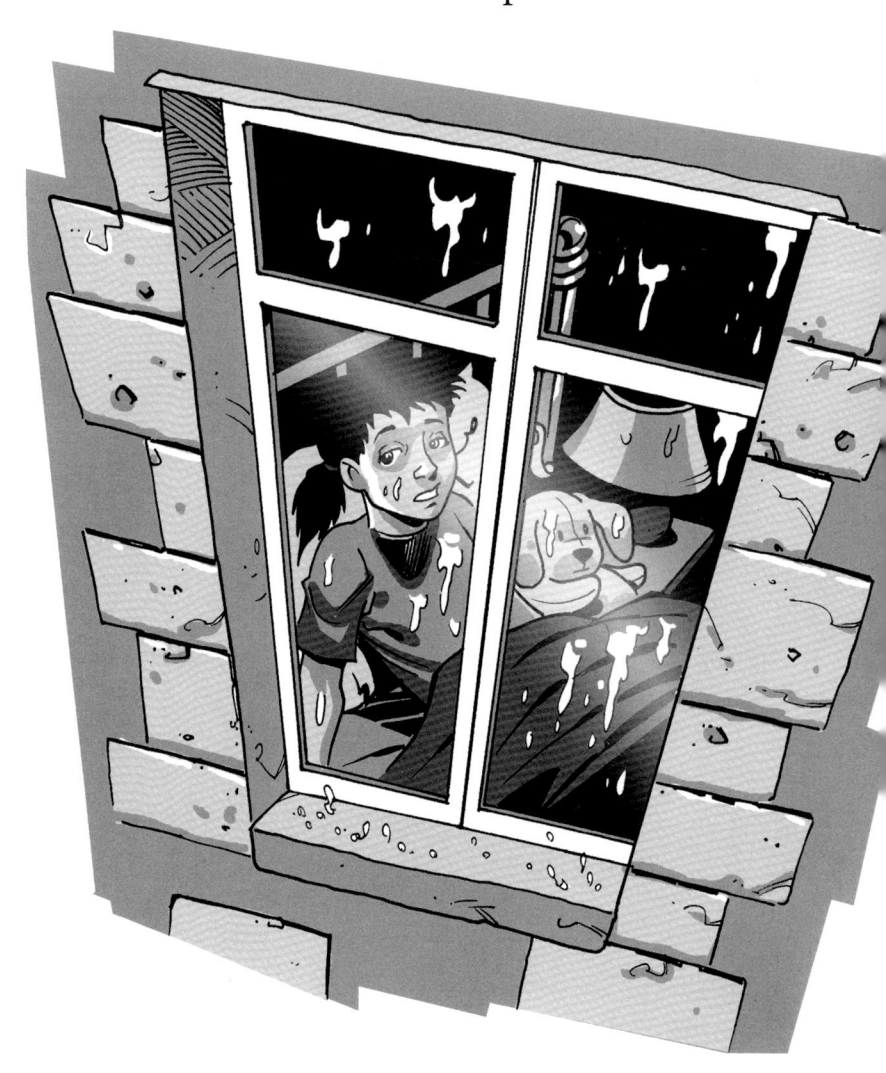

She looked out of the window.

She saw a light.

She pulled on her coat and boots and looked outside.

CHAPTER 3
THIEF

Teresa saw a light in one of the tunnels.

"It's the strawberry thief!" she said.

She phoned the police.

The thief did not hear the police arrive.
The rain on the tunnels was too loud!

The police woke up the farmer.
Then they took away the thief.

The farmer was not cross with Teresa.

He said, "Teresa can eat all the strawberries she wants."

Questions:

Where did the family work?

What was the weather like on the night Teresa saw a light?

How many policemen came to catch the thief?

What did the farmer say to Teresa after the thief had been caught?

A Different Life

by Alison Hawes

Illustrated by Anthony Williams

Contents

Chapter 1
The Move   19

Chapter 2
Different   22

Chapter 3
The Same!   28

Questions   32

Vocabulary:

Different   Language
Weather   Home
Job   War

Main characters:

Sofia

Omar

Mum

Dad

Chapter 1
The Move

"Life will be different here," say Mum and Dad.

"The people look different," says Omar.

"And the language is different," says Sofia.

Chapter 2
Different

"Our home is different," says Mum.

"And the weather is different," says Dad.

"The shops look different," says Mum.

"And the food is different," says Sofia.

"My job is different," says Dad.

"Our school looks different," say Omar and Sofia.

Chapter 3
The Same!

"But the football is the same!" says Omar

"And the basketball is the same!" says Sofia.

"Life is different here," say Mum and Dad. "Life here is good."

"Yes," say Omar and Sofia. "Life here is good!"

Questions:

What is Sofia reading in Chapter 1?

What kind of weather is Dad dressed for in Chapter 2?

What sport is the same for Omar?

What sport is the same for Sofia?

Is the family happy with their new life?